Self-Portraits Ex Machina
(No. —, US, No. America)

poems by

Devi S. Laskar

Finishing Line Press
Georgetown, Kentucky

Self-Portraits
Ex Machina
(No. —, US, No. America)

Copyright © 2025 by Devi S. Laskar
ISBN 979-8-89990-280-2 First Edition
All rights reserved under International and Pan-American Copyright Conventions. No part of this book may be reproduced in any manner whatsoever without written permission from the publisher, except in the case of brief quotations embodied in critical articles and reviews.

Publisher: Leah Huete de Maines
Editor: Christen Kincaid
Cover Art: Devi S. Laskar
Author Photo: Anjini Laskar
Cover Design: Elizabeth Maines McCleavy

Order online: www.finishinglinepress.com
also available on amazon.com

Author inquiries and mail orders:
Finishing Line Press
PO Box 1626
Georgetown, Kentucky 40324
USA

Contents

In This Game of *Sorry*, You Never Apologize 1
Though the Stars Walk Backward 3
Particles of Speech 5
Raga 7
Self-Portrait Near the Stars & Stripes… 8
Vacation Bible School, 1977 10
Sounding Off… 11
Aunt-By-Marriage 12
Self-Portrait: Chapel Hill, N.C. 13
While the mayfly bombards the river reeds… 15
Self-Portrait Near the Regal Cinema…. 16
Untitled Western Country Song… 17
Some words… 18
Departure Terminal 20
On Sadness 21
Self-Portrait Outside the U.S. District… 22
Chord & discord 23
Routes 24
Measuring the Weight of your Smile 25
Self-Portrait with Rearview Mirror 27
Notes from the Post-Colonial Cookbook 28
Scratch 29
Self-Portrait With Child 30
Restaurant Queue Contrapuntal 31
The All-Saints, XX, Overeaters Support Group 34
Self-Portrait with Bathroom Mirror… 36
Unanswered, untranslatable 39
Self-Portrait with Fun House Reflection… 40
Why I _____ 42
Self-Portrait at Divination Conference 44

For my family

In This Game Of *Sorry*, You Never Apologize

(For E., B., T., W., R., K., E.A., D., G.)

1.

Late to this game of *Clue* only it'll never be
the professor with a candlestick in the parlor, now
the drywall stands half done. Some stranger will hold
up the photograph of your mother, miles before
you were conceived, tiles bloodied on the kitchen floor.

2.

Late to this game of Charades, Lizzie already making
out with the pizza delivery man in the alcove,
the neighbor's kid put his cheese sandwich in the fish tank
and now the gold is belly up. Someone's dialed the volume
so loud to *Fantasy Island* that when Tattoo yells
out "the plane the plane" all you can do is take cover
and hope the world doesn't come crashing down.

3.

Late to this game of Spin the Bottle, Go-Laap already
drunk and from where she stands on the veranda the moon
is a ribbon in her cumulus cloud of hair.
Still hours before she will test the laws of gravity, learn
whether you can un-break a broken hand—your future
mother-in-law will label her as picture perfect.

4.

Late to this game of *Monopoly*: did you know
you can go straight to jail and not collect $200 right
here at the Woolworth's counter? When will you learn
that the man you crushed on was off-duty five-o,
taking a spin with a stranger's great white fins?

5.

Late to this game of Hide & Seek, some girls will hole
up in the fields for 50 years and emerge as snakes
or long walking sticks because that's what a half
century of silence will do to the body.

6.

Late to this game of Poker, all one big bluff
so you can buy your fruit by the pound, so you don't
have to take a bite out of the one poisoned apple,
so you don't have to wait for some colonizer's son
to kiss your painted lips and make you feel alive.

7.

Early to this game of *Life*, there are only
two people living outside Eden right now
and the multitudes who will birth ships and sky-
scrapers and guns and cactus, bees and lipstick
and a parliament of owls haven't been born yet.

8.

Early to this game of *Name that Tune*, the contestants
are still in the street crewing for graffiti clubs and break-
dancing troupes, siphoning rhymes from the radio,
their bodies as hard as a pea must have felt to the princess
sleeping on a stack of mattresses. Please don't ever
again conflate myths with lies. Jam is just another
word for jelly, just the third beat after traffic.

9.

Early to this perennial game of *Hangman*: all
that separates cool from coo is the L in love.

Though the stars walk backward

People worry over it as if it were a heavy object,
Atlas carrying the world on his back, always
a black and white sketch of the yoked oxen
next to the definition in the illustrated dictionary—

Atlas carrying the world on his back, always
it is as big and small as you wish it to be,
next to the definition in the illustrated dictionary.
The roll of the years and the quick tick of the hours.

It is as big and small as you wish it to be:
a thin scratch where the skin is torn open,
the roll of the hours and the quick tick of the years
and at once a gash that scars, requiring stitches.

A thin scratch where the skin is torn open.
Carry it as if were a dream, half-remembered,
and at once a gash that scars requiring stitches
silvery around the measures, sometimes sweet.

Carry it as if it were a dream, half-remembered,
carry it as if it were a song, auld lang syne
silvery around the measures, sometimes sweet—
your tongue tripping over the last line.

Carry it as if it were a song, auld lang syne,
carry it the way a tree would carry it,
your tongue tripping over the last line
all bark, all roots, all sticky gold sap.

Carry it the way a tree would carry it,
stooping to it but not breaking its boughs—
all bark, all roots, all sticky gold sap.
Carry it as if you had life expectancy

stooping to it but not breaking its boughs;
and freedom of an ocean breeze:
Carry it as if you had life expectancy
and a sunset to look forward to

and freedom of an ocean breeze.
A black and white sketch of the yoked oxen
And a sunset to look forward to.
People worship it as if it were a heavy object.

Particles of speech

1.
In English, midnight is syntactic
rather than inflectional since
there is no specific midnight verb form:

I midnight   We midnight
You midnight   You midnight
She midnights They midnight

2.
But in every Bengali
household, there's noon at every meal:

Noon is salt

3.
Every time she asks me to pass the tin
cup of kosher crystals I check my watch
and correct the dissolving time

4.
Maaj rath is midnight

5.
There's no place like midnight
There's no place like maaj rath
There's no place like midnight

6.
Maaj rath sweet midnight
Sweet midnight maaj rath
Midnight maaj rath sweet

7.
In Bangla, one says o-there baaro-ta
bey-jey-chey when someone encounters
top of the line misfortune

8.
Their clock has struck twelve

9.
I laugh when I have to translate
what she says, but I have never
once asked which 12.

10.
Scientists argue that midnight
already occupies every atom,
that the magic of our bodies
is nothing but the crush of sky
canvas, clouds and stardust.

11.
What if midnight is a devout
clockmaker, granting us prayer
as thin hands clasp together
in the moment between today
and the start of tomorrow?

12.
Evie is right, the more midnight
you have, the more you want.

Raga

Forget the red dust-swept avenues, the drumbeat of your heart, the taxis jiggling over cobbled stones; dodging pedestrians and rickshaws in the opposing lanes, the naked street men bathing at public pumps, their street wives squatting in every busy doorway. Forget them all begging for charity and spare change. Forget the decay of dead palaces of the Raj; the ordinary people who cleverly squat there, now; and that they hang their laundry like a lynching mob. Forget hawkers peddling mustard seed oil and green bananas. Forget the congested sewers: urchins and rats now fight for the trash and spittle you pitch out the window; the narrowing alleys and closing minds, the buildings stacked and pushed against each other like gaily dressed children in a queue. Forget the little blue and red awnings of skinny tin-thatched stalls, the leering smiles of vendors whose eyes you catch and meet, the diesel perfume wafting through your open window, the winter sun glaring on the dashboard, the clamor of commercial planes overhead. Forget the bellow of buses as they stream past you, angry as a stampede of mechanical bulls; your insomnia as the moon casts ghosts behind you, the ashen taste of the Ganges water under your tongue. Forget the roar of men and women everywhere as they feud, and that they brawl in public over everything and nothing and you. Forget you're visiting red fire ants, in a bay colony. Forget it all, the sounds of crows feeding and mating, mating and feeding; your appetite, which you lost weeks ago at an open market as the butcher conducted his last transaction for the day. Remember to watch a street boy bring a bag of stolen oranges to his ailing mother in that neglected grotto. Remember to empty your pockets into the hundred open palms praying for change at every corner. Remember there's no substitute for love or hunger, nothing I say will ever quell your feverish heat, your thirst. Remember me always when I leave here. Wait. Where do you think you're going?

((Haibun) Self-Portrait Near the Stars & Stripes, (Three Rows Back, Leftmost Column)(Hard Chairs With Boxy Desks Bolted To Its Legs)(Mrs. Stillwell's Homeroom,)(Erasers Cleaned, Chalkboard Blank, Green-Black Rectangle)(Catholic Elementary School With Convent Attached)(the Middle & High Schools Built Years Later) (the Diocese Would Buy All the Surrounding Forest On That Side of 15-501 By-Pass, Resurrect the Future Felled Trees, Reincarnate Them Into a Rectory & Weekday Shelter)(Wednesday Morning)(Winter) (Dressed in Green-Black-Red Plaid School Uniform & Horrible Mother-Approved White Sweater With Grape Juice Stain That Won't Come Out)(One Of the Sisters Had Already Rapped Your Hand With a Blond Wooden Ruler the Day Before, For Falling Asleep During American History)(You Weren't Asleep, You Were Readjusting Your Eyes, You Were Trying to Un-See the Trail Of Tears Drawings In the History Textbook,)(Per President Jackson's Indian Removal Act of 1830)(Nine American States & Territories Largely Extinguishing) (Through Relocation and Death March)(the Cherokee, Creek, Chickasaw, Choctaw and Seminole Nations and Countless Smaller Tribes)(Total of 5045 Miles of Trails Over Land and Water)(Toward the Dustbowls of Oklahoma)(It was Liam Who Made a Joke About Removing You, If You Weren't Careful)(You Were Trying Not To Cry) (You Wondered If This School and Your House Were Built on Unceded Cherokee Lands,)(You Went Home and Looked in the Encyclopedia, Found An Entry About the Occaneechi-Saponi People Who Once Dwelled in Orange County)(a Different Sister, Thick Spectacles and Thicker Eyebrows, Commands Everyone To Rise)(the Others Have Laid Their Palms Over Their Hearts)(the Others Have Opened Their Mouths In Rote Recitation)(Pledge Of Allegiance)(...'To the Republic For Which It Stands, One Nation Under God, Indivisible...')(the Oath Dries In Your Throat)(Your Hand Falls To Your Side As You Consider the Term You Heard Your Father Say To Your Mother, About Locating the Nearest Nota Republic)(You Wonder How Soon Your Family Will Have To Move To the Land of No-Ta)(And If They Even Speak English There)(Liam Leaves His Row And Column, and Marches Straight For You)("Put Your Hand Over Your Heart," He Hisses)(His Eyes Dark With Anger)(You Shake Your Head)(You Remember Your Mother Mispronouncing Liam's Name During Back-To-School Night)('Who Names Their Son, Lie Am?')(the Spectacled Sister Comes Toward You, Ruler In Hand, Sneezing)) Fifth Grade—Chapel Hill, NC 1977

God bless you.
God only knows what happens next.

Vacation Bible School, 1977

Kool-Aid purpling the water in the clear glass
pitcher; waxy lips of the Dixie cups; the crunch
of salt and vinegar potato chips

during the breaks—forbidden food at home
but freely consumed in the Sunday school rooms

above the rectory; the comic books
revealing Jesus as magician, able
to feed five thousand with a few fish and crusty

loaves of stale bread. Still, I was sent home after
the second week for my faithless math. Where

did all the people come from if Eve the only
woman? The rest of my summer Eden
of my own making, stealing blush-red apples

from the Thompsons' tree, biking to the highway
overpass and chucking the hard-chewed cores

past the chain-link fence to the road below,
waiting for the next motorist to flatten
any evidence of my new-found knowledge.

Sounding off

Sari silk sarcophagus but not the cadaver's
dissected esophagus. Trembling but only when
the treble clef is obvious. The blue violence

of indigo, the mistaken identity
of forget-me-nots. Arterial hearts of peaches.

The click clack of the neighbor's dog on the stairs.
The click clack click of the train on the railroad built

when my grandfather was only a boy. The eyes,
the ayes, the 'I's always have it. Always halve it.
Sunflowers wet on the canvas. Sunflowers etched

at the bottom of the serving dish. Sunflowers
asleep in winter refusing to rise under

weak dawning. Champagne because the 'g' is silent.
Quatrain because the 'q' is not. Mascarpone

and julienne mandolin in every TV cook's
kitchen. Scotch whiskey dares and picture brides in
the war stories we hear. Every tale turns into Hades's

abduction of Persephone. Her mother's abject
grief and how the leaves burned copper and bronze. How

the leaves fell one by two, faster and faster until
everything, the world, was found wanting at her feet.

Aunt-by-Marriage

A few things I know about the ones
who came before you and paved the road
you now stand on: theirs was a blue world
tinged with stoicism and guilt.

Who came before you and paved the road
with unnamed humiliations, marriages,
tinged with stoicism and guilt
and children who glimmered immortality?

With unnamed humiliations, marriages,
as they played among the tall grass;
children who glimmered immortality:
they had mornings where there was nothing

as they played among the tall grass
to swallow their own yellowed anger.
They had mornings where there was nothing,
their faces masks of calm as they tended

to swallow their own yellowed anger—
manage the stove, the cradle, ruined men;
their faces masks of calm as they tended
to broken bottles, their tears, lost jewelry.

They managed the stove, the cradle, ruined men
you now stand on: theirs was a blue world
over broken bottles, their tears, lost jewelry—
a few things I know about the ones.

((Haibun) Self-Portrait (In Between Old Well and The Bell, But Closer To the Latter)(Near The Pit And the Off-Color Posters Pinned To the Carousel Kiosks Proclaiming Pseudonym R.E.M.'s Anticipated Arrival On Franklin Street,)(On a Monday or Thursday Afternoon)(Inside Greenlaw—the Multi-Media Building In Proximity Of Lenoir Hall, the Dungeon & Dragon Of University Cafeterias)(Lunch Had Been a Solitary Endeavor (XL Styrofoam Cup Of Coffee With Three Sugars & Two Percent Milk Followed By One Greasy Grilled Cheese Sandwich)) (and the Glare Of Work-Study Students Busing the Nearby Tables, and Collecting the Detritus Of a Hive of Identically Dressed Greek-Lettered Girls Who Had Deposited Their Garbage and Trays Where They Sat Before They Exited)(Second To Last Row Of the Congested Viewing Room, In Between the Wall and the Emergency Use Only Door)(Every Seat Occupied)(the Instructor's Warning About the Content Of the Historically Significant 'First' Modern Movie)(Considered a Pioneer Of Close-Ups, Fade Outs and Use of Extras (Many In Blackface)) (First 12-Reel Film, First Film To Introduce Intermission, First (Silent) Film To Host a Live Orchestra To Render the Musical Score) (Film Credited For Birthing ____ Renaissance in America)(Woodrow Wilson, Georgia Native & Father Of League Of Nations Which Led To the Naissance Of the United Nations, Was a Fan)(First Film To Ever Be Screened At the White House)(Your T.A.'s Warning That To Leave Before the 180-Minute Motion Picture Ran Its Course Would Result In (Dire) Consequences (Grade Plummeting, Credit Revoking)) (Only 6 Years Before the Library Of Congress Deems It (Culturally) (Historically)(Aesthetically) Significant))(Only 7 Years Before It Is Made Part Of the National Film Registry)(Only 12 Years Before The American Film Institute Names It Among the 100 Best Films Of the Century, Citing Its Director As 'Shakespeare Of the Screen')(32 Years Before Your Classmate Christine Testifies Before Congress Ahead Of a SCOTUS Appointment)(And 32 Years Before the Silent Sam Statue Is (Finally) Removed For Good (But the First Female Chancellor Carol Is Forced Out Of Office))(35 Years Before the Pulitzer-Prize Winning Alumna Nikole Is Not (Initially) Offered Tenure)) With Eyes Closing During the Opening Credits and Opening (When Fraternity Brothers On the First Row Laugh) and Closing (and Closing); Chapel Hill (On the Campus of the Nation's First Public University)), NC (—1986)

God, forbid.
God forbid.
God forbid.

**While the mayfly bombards the river reeds
on his first and last day, the (usually male)
first-, second- and thousandth- journalism
instructor and/or English & composition teacher
and/or assistant city editor tells you to keep it
short and write so the dominant culture audience
doesn't know you're a girl & a girl of color at that…**

you want me to consider
the ephemeral light in which

I rise to this moment's occasion;
you caution me not to interrupt

the physics within—the sinew
of skin and muscle, bone levers

and vein pulleys—the throng of red
blood cells congregating

in the service of one prayer.
my only job, you say, is to cast

the fisherman waiting
by the river's edge

and find sequins to play
the part of the evening stars.

(Haibun) Self-Portrait Near the Regal Cinema Bell Tower (on Regal Parkway)(The Assistant To the Assistant City Planner Really Has No Memory/History/Courage/Imagination Whatsoever, Both Rosa Parks and Henry Aaron Were On the Shortlist)(You Really Have To Do a Story About This Sometime,)(Between McGregor Boulevard That Will Have 24-hour Construction Crews & Equipment On It For the Next Four Months (For a Single F$ck&ng Pothole The Size Of a Silver Dollar,)(You Really Have To Do a Story About That Sometime))(and Big Pine Way Where There is Not One But Two Hooters in Between the Chuck E. Cheese and the Circle-K (It's Like 7-Eleven Only Less Secure, Eight Female Clerks, All Black or Latina, Have Been Shot at Six Different Locations In the Last Three Weeks and You're So Damn Tired Of Asking the Sheriff What Extra Security Measures Are Being Put In Place and Has Anyone Been Arrested For These Murders?)) (You Loathe That Smarmy Smile He Gives You After His Eyes Take a Lunch Break On Your Chest)(Across the Street, Practically, From the Manmade Lake That Abuts Thomas Edison's Winter Home (Built a Century Before You Even Began Working In This Godless Swamp, and Admission Costs Too Much To Hide Out in Regularly When You're Trying To Get Away From Your Executive City Editor's Beef-Fajita-Laced Scolding))(Yes, Him, the One Who Looks Like Jabba the Hutt's Younger Brother and Who Doesn't Like Women and Hates Women Of Color Even More)(Especially After They Don't Accept His Dinner Invitations)(Especially After They Don't Laugh At His Flatulent Jokes) (and He Is Trying So Hard To Move You To the F$ck&ng Bonita Springs Bureau Where You'd Have To Share an Office With Melissa Holiday Who Smokes Clove Cigarettes and Drinks Tequila Sunrises on the Job and, Come To Think Of It, Is FckNG the Aforementioned Executive City Editor On the Weekends Because Haven't You Spotted Them Coming Out Of That Coral-Colored Single-Story Motel Near the Caloosahatchee, Next To Page Field?)(You Really Wish You Could Do a Story About That One Day))—Ft. Myers, FL (Don't Spell Out Fort In the City Name Again, You'll Get Fired Next Time!) 1989

God, I hate the smell of yesterday's popcorn.
God, I know all the dialogue in *Working Girl*.

Untitled Western Country Song in Rubescent A Minor

pigment and refraction, the way our bees don't see red, strawberries kissing in a sun-dried field, a ditty on the radio about Graceland, root-beer-glazed chicken over a gluten-free waffle, hip hip chin chin

in a ruffled tulle skirt, sunrise smokestacks near the estuary as cirriform clouds rubberneck, that drunk woman in the gravel lot parking too close,

Dixie pickup the color of tail-lights with a gun rack, a distortion of old glory unfurling in its unmade bed, bedraggled dianthus and plastic peonies at the gold rush churchyard, sprinklers going awry, the way our dogs don't

see red, aspens testing theoretical immortality, video arcades boarding neon vacancy signs, convex lips, an evaporating lake, *All in the Family reruns*,

million women marches, red-tail shark tank, Sanskrit psalms read from a red leather bound book, the front man holds a red guitar he cannot play, misspelled henna tattoos, dog-eared clovers amid the poppies, that drunk

woman inserting her room key into your back pocket, cathedrals of traffic jams and stop signs, a ruby-throated monologue about chainsaws watched

through bloodshot eyes, sea crests of cinnamon toothpaste & farm troughs, the Sicilian lasagna I cook but cannot eat, the way our fathers have stopped seeing red, two dollars short of a bacon and eggs midnight diner breakfast,

that drunk woman tripping over rubicund spike heels, zinnias blossoming in her cheeks, blood roses' ticker-tape parade, do you really believe

the summer will never end? God love you lass, God love your ass.

Some words will be repeated at least twice, some three times like a mantra, some words are there for the free food and some words are sitting in the back row, trying to start a forest fire

Splatter	Static	Superfluous	Skinny
Spent	Sum	Saddened	Solace
Shards	Sinister	Storm	Shards
Steel-cut	Shame	Sedentary	Silence
Sari	Seismology	Stark	Standard
Stale	Saturate	Stupidity	Scour

1. S is for radio _____, not knowing the _____ of the out_____ world's ailments, cluster upon cluster of broken moments and deaths, when the world was at war and war was _____ with famine.

2. S is for the _____ never lasting long enough in the emptied Ovaltine jars for the ants to get in: my Didu _____ it over _____ and _____ di_____s alike, because _____ _____, how will enjoy the _____ without tasting a bit of the _____ underneath? My Dadu's voice echoing from the other room, we are so lucky to have _____ at all, because there was a time before you were born, when your mother was a _____ little girl, that there was no _____ at all. Using a teaspoon to measure out _____ heaps until the glass jar was only holding Kolkata air and _____ to the open pump next to the koi pond to be wa___d.

3. S is for the _____ little girl who later became my mother, the girl who grew up to have a big _____ tooth, a girl who remained _____ throughout the years and could not abide my fat. S is for the _____ girl who grew up and got married and had kids of her own, and moved to America and had American dollars in her purse and could eat what _____ liked and was never _____. Because that kind of _____ never goes away.

4. S is for *Mary Poppins*, and watching the movie again and again, the children cleaning up their rooms while _____ _____ A _____ of _____; wishing I could _____ my fingers to have the toy _____ march themselves back into the chambers of their deep chest.

5. S is for the ancient porcelain _____, chipped on one _____, matching cup broken and long retired to the landfill on which rested a few _____ chilies and wedges of lemon, the kind that gave off the best _____ but wasn't too _____.

6. S is for the _____ from the _____, large crystal formations flavoring all of the food put before us, often on wide _____ of banana leaves: the mango lentil soup, the tiny fish in pungent curries with names longer than their lengths from top to toe, it was years before my parents would realize the fish they craved so much in India was called buffalo carp in America, and that it was considered black food in their tiny _____ hamlet, that most of the white people didn't even know what to do with it.

7. S is for _____ Wars playing at the Varsity theater playing 8000 miles away, a movie my mother vows never to let me _____ because galactic battles and the death _____ are examples of witchcraft.

8. S is for _____ out with my friends and _____ing it for myself.

9. S is for another _____ afternoon at my grandparents' house, the _____ girls rinsing the dishes with extra care because my father was coming to lunch, Jamai Babu, the _____-in-law.

10. S is for _____, the way my grandmother would _____ when her _____-in-law would say to her I don't have enough money to come back with your daughter next year for a visit—her _____ _____, and _____ would always reply, "_____ what you can do. _____ you _____." And he always managed to bring her back. _____ was right.

Departure terminal

Not a spirited game of *Chutes & Ladders*
nor a spin at the roulette wheel; or leaving

your house for the last time, only the phone book
and dictionary left unpacked. But you turning

the knob of the kaleidoscope even when
you knew it was broken, pretending to see

something new in that tired face of the moon.
Not the stars taking a tumble on the dark

carpet of night but instead, resuming their
rightful positions by morning — replacing

our wishes for what could be with what is. Salt
crystals scatter on black granite countertop,

a map of constellations to flavor our last
supper. Let's promise to remember our stories

even as our tongues temper and cure, even
as we start to forget each other's proper names.

On sadness

I want to tell you
a story, about something
that's important to you:
the fruit falling
far or close to its tree—
the shape the bruises
assume, how the dents
turn purple after a day
or two. Most people
ignore things with bruises
on them, aubergine
the color of imperfection.
It looks good on me.
I wear your sorrow well.

**

I wear your sorrow well.
It looks good on me,
the color of imperfection.
On them, aubergine.
Ignore things with bruises
or two. Most people
turn purple after a day,
assume how, the dents,
the shape, the bruises.
Far or close to its tree
the fruit falling.
That's important to you:
A story, about something
I want to tell you.

(Haibun) Self-Portrait Outside the U.S. District Courthouse in Vermilion County (Leave It To the Good People of Central Illinois To Have Named This Province After the Most Toxic Mineral Known To Man)( )(A.K.A. Cinnabar, A.K.A. Mercury Sulfide)(Twelve Hours After Spotting Three Crosses Burning a Hole In the Night Sky On a Not-Too-Distant Hill Off I-74)(Not More Than a 2-Minute Drive From You Now Stand)(Minutes After Telling Your Editor-In-Chief "The Klan is Here")(Who Left His Cushy Job in Central FL To Move With His Wife (Your Good Friend For the Past Year) And Three Kids Back To His 'Hometown' Newspaper)(Who (After Closing The Door To His Glass Office, Put His Hand On Your Shoulder and Offered You a Striped Butter Mint And a Day Off In the Not-Too-Distant Future When He's Hired A Few More Good Reporters Like You) Said "No, They're Not,"))(You Taste the Red Tide Churn Of Algae On Your Tongue, You Recall It Was a Full Moon Last Night)(Isaac Newton Once Said the Full Moon Affected The Ocean Water Inside the Human Body, Causing Epilepsy, Kidney Stones and Menstrual Cycles—You Look Closely At Your Editor and Wonder Which Of Those Conditions He is Experiencing)(Followed By the Most Damning Thing a Newspaper Man Can Say, "We Shouldn't Rock the Boat.")(Leave It To the Good People To Have Adopted the Northern Cardinal As the State Bird When They Should Have Demanded Ostrich)(Not to Be Too Picky, But You Both Know Central Illinois is Practically Land-Locked)(You Swallow The Mint Whole and Start To Choke, Run Into The Bathroom Down The Hall to Put Your Fingers Down Your Throat,)(Like The Who Song,)(You Remember the Sindoor, the Vermilion Powder Hindu Women, Married Hindu Women, Put In the Part Of Their Hair)(To Denote Their Marriage Status to Society)(You Remember Reading There Is Unsafe Amounts of Lead In the Powder Your Mother and Grandmothers and Aunts and Cousins and Friends Use)(You Think Back To the FDA Analysis and the CDC Warning, That Lead Exposure Leads To I.Q. Loss, Attention Deficit, Leading To Loss of Academic Achievement)(Then Hyperventilate Before Grabbing Your Keys and Heading Back Outside)) Waiting For The Verdict To Come In (On a Totally Unrelated Search & Seizure Case, You're Sure) —Danville, IL 1990

God, I quit.
God, I'm broke.

Chord & discord

Not a cord of wood, chopped and stacked
outside. Not a tiny cluster of
letters strummed on the refurbished
guitar. Not a lifeline across

the karma circle between two
points at its circumference. Blush
instead like an oyster. Never
let them see the pearls of your teeth,

never let them hear you butcher
their mother tongue; and instantly
understand that you don't know how
to bargain, that you can't afford

the high cost of their bitter gourd,
that you must leave their song unfinished.

Routes

the whole
story
of migration
lies
in a curried
English
translation.
What is
the seesaw
between roots
and routes?
One
binds us
to the ground
where trees
are born.
The other
frees us
to follow
the sound
of Fall
approaching,
the sight
of geese
flapping
heart-beat
wings.

Measuring the weight of your smile

What's before you all I have to show—
not much more than a buck campfire
and a tired spit upon which to cook the maize.
Nothing keeps company like a rooster
that has no occupation except to run
and preside over my copper-bottomed scale.

Proof of my love will hardly tip any scale:
as if stolen candies and siphoned gas show
I am anything more than a girl on the run,
with a fondness for poppies, breathing fire
and plagiarizing the nearest rooster
that has mapped a way out of the maze.

Like Scheherazade, I tell tales that can amaze
yet bear out my virginity on your tight-lipped scale;
my questions cannot be heard over your rooster
that is drowned out by the ex-girlfriend's sparklers show.
Nothing's worse than your dissenting vote: Fire
the messengers, track their shadows as they run.

I muster your wants like a congressional run,
practicing diplomacy as you promote maize
over my homegrown remedies, over-egging the fire
just to see the limo and hear Pavarotti scale
three octaves as he warms up before the show.
I prefer to eat nothing rather than raw or live rooster.

Before the serenade, I scavenge for a lattice rooster
but find only a purpled weathervane overrun
with rust; I write an aubade when you fail to show.
I am a mural made of multi-colored maize,
a cautionary tale hidden in the chapel doors. Scale
back the lens to witness the exquisite corpse on fire.

From a distance, the diamonds in her lobes catch like fire
as a fancied new macaw debuts in front of my rooster.
I am a fish, its body weighed and indentured; no scale,
silver coins for the ferryman, left upon me. I'll run
over you next time in another courtship resembling a maze.
This understudy will learn her lines before the next show.

The design of the city scale model does not show
that it is the year of the rooster, the maize
must be hidden for a time when fate cannot be outrun.

((Haibun) Self-Portrait Near Ralph D. Abernathy Road (Though You Haven't Seen a Person Of Color Who Doesn't Wait At the Bus Stop at Night In, What, Three Months?)(and Roswell Road)(You Once Drove Toward the Heralded Suburb For Which the Road is Named, Just to Count (1) the Number Of Signs Proudly Proclaiming What Good Ancestors Lived There Because They Didn't Discriminate (Offering Medical Aid To the Union- and Confederate- Soldiers Alike)((13) and For That, General Sherman's Troops Spared Them When They Burned Down Atlanta) and (2) The Number of Betsy Ross Flags Still Saluting the Contemporary Sky With Its 13—Point 'New Constellation' Configuration)((1777)(the Number and the Year)(You Really Should Do a Story About That Sometime))(By March Creek)(See (1))(While Being Pulled Over In What Can Only Be Described As a Tsunami of Late June Sun-In-Your-Eyes Daylight the Afternoon After the Strawberry Moon Has Glazed the Near-Term Horizon)(45 Minutes Past the Moment When Not One Not Two But Three Ladies Of a Certain Age Yell At the Store Manager Because You Wouldn't Go To the Back and Check the Stock and You Don't Even Work There)(You Were Just Shopping in a F$ck&ng Fire Engine Red T-shirt and the Only Other Girls Of Color Are Employees in Cherry Red Vests)(and Said Ladies Wouldn't Apologize & Kept Insisting the Manager Had To Let You Go and To Never Again Hire a Girl Like You,)(a Girl Who Could Sass Like That, What With the Olympic Games Coming To Town Next Month,)(and You Actually Didn't Say a Word, But As the Saying Goes, If Looks Could Kill, Well There'd Be Three Less Shopping at K-Mart)(After the Aviator-Shaded Deputy Turns On His Lights and Bullhorn)(After He Sees Your Press Badge Dangling From a Chain Like an Air-Freshener) (After He Asks You If You're a Reporter and You Answer Yes)(After He Asks You What Beat You Cover, and For Fun You Answer Police (True But False, Cops Yes, Fulton County, No))(After He Hands You Back Your License and Registration and Backs Away as If You're a Body On Fire and Leaves *Sans* Issuance of Speeding Citation)) With Rearview Mirror (—Unincorporated Sandy Springs, GA 1996))

God! Help me.
God, help me.
God help me.

Notes from the Post-Colonial Cookbook

This ____ draws loosely, like apron strings, from _____ stories of cooking, famine, hunger, open flames and recipes. Also, it references specific dates and memories that remain unresolved & unwritten:

Title Poem: The bouillabaisse was served in a basin-shaped ceramic bowl, but what you remember is the taste of the sea, its brine, its longevity.

Page 8: Noon is salt. And Tuesdays and Saturdays are good days to fast. The holy woman cried when she read your astral forecast, and you took it to mean there would be years of questions answered with rain-soaked afternoons.

Page 7: Liam showed you the cabinet where the blood of Christ (for kids) was kept, mimed his thirst. And you both drank the forbidden grape juice, greedily.

Page 14: "Are You trying to poison yourself?" She asked. "You know, cheese is mold."

Page 17: When they look at you they see too much.

Page 30: You once dropped your baby tooth into a glass of root beer and watched is dissolve and disappear, like magic.

Page 25: In English, the preferred vegetable is called Chinese bitter gourd. You found out at the International Farmers Market in DeKalb, a thousand immigrants waiting in line for the cashiers, clinging to their origin stories as if their lives depended on it.

Page 34: Rasugolla dreams—via ___.

Page 48: You still wait for the taste of life to return. Also, you crave all the things you cannot __.

Page 49: Bear in mind, to finish it one must crush cardamom and black pepper and cinnamon stick.

Page 53: You ___ to remember.

Scratch

I call to have my mother translate the recipe
from her grandmother, the one who married
at nine, had my *Grand* before she turned a baker's
dozen. Ma speaks in her native tongue, saltwater

in her throat, warns me to remember to sugar
sparingly and curdle the milk without scorching
the pan. I cradle the phone in one hand as I
squeeze the lemon wedges drop by drop into

the boil, and wait for it to change to dough.
"The syrup you'll make only looks simple," she says.
"You don't have the patience." She is right of
course; I am glad an hour later that she couldn't

smell my burnt failures wafting from the kitchen
sink, nor watch me eat dessert from a can.

((Haibun) Self-Portrait (at Morgan Falls State Park, Less Than a Mile (4000 Feet To Be Precise) From the Once Pristine Chattahoochee River, Near the Fulton-Cobb Border)(Near the As Yet Un-Ravished Bull Sluice and Orkin Lakes)(the Almost Indecipherable Smell, At Once Rotten Egg, At Once Sweet Benzene Fumes Of the Devil Making a Stop in Georgia) (Though No Fiddles Could Be Heard,)(the Sound of Back Hoes In the Distance Competing With the Voices Of White Men Speaking Into a Bank Of Microphones,)(Politicians and Pipeline Officials (the Names Of the Companies Doing Business, Colonial and Plantation)(Though It Was Colonial's Spill In This Particular Instance)(Though It Was Thought To Be Gasoline It Wasn't Clear What Was Passing Through) (From TX to NJ, Today:)(The Question Had a Multiple Choice Answer: Natural Gas, Oil, Diesel, Kerosene, Jet Fuel, Carbon Dioxide) Alike With Equal Volume, Distancing Themselves From Each Other As the NTSB Excavated the Crime Scene to Determine Where to Lay Blame.) (It Would Later Be Reported and Proved: a 30,000 Gallon Spill,) (Parabola Of Apartment Dwellers and Longtime Residents Displaced,) (At This Moment, Everyone Looking Up At the Pewter Clouds Everyone Knowing That the Coming Rains Would Bring Floods,) (Knowing That Floods Would Cause the Dams to Spill Over and Flood the Tributaries)(Knowing That Floods Would Affect the Drinking Water Supply)(Later, Much Later, You Would Come to Know How the Pipeline, Already 20 Years Old and Un-Parented, Had Buckled and Cracked, How Refuse From A Nearby Trash Depository Had Crept In) (It Would Be Another Decade Before Saidiya Would Write Her Essay and Another 13 Years Before You Read In Her Words, The Question, 'What Do Stories Afford Anyway?')(The Hatch of Caddis Flies and Mayflies In Your Periphery, and The Anglers With Weathered Skin)(Muttering In the Crowd)(Stepping Away,)(There Was Still Time In the Evening Rise, To Catch The Fish Before the Gasoline Steeped In the Ground Like Black Tea, Staining the Water Table Forever)) With Child (You Cannot Stand Any Longer, You Must Rest Soon, You Cannot Lose Another Baby, You Cannot—)) —Unincorporated North Fulton County, GA 1998

God, not here.
God, I'm going to throw up.
God not here.

Restaurant Queue Contrapuntal

It's all I can hold	in my mouth
thrashing	hungry birds
my stomach	rumbling
percussion	
for what I want to	say but don't
the hostess	
	nodding
but	
not writing	down
my name	on the list
the hostess seating	the couple behind me
	in line.
The birds	
in my mouth	scratching
	my tongue
	with their talons
their beaks	beginning
to	
type	a Morse code of
dashes	
and	
	ellipses.
These birds	
	of impatience
These birds	that have been
wounded,	
These birds	that have
ascended from	their righteous hunger
the hostess	seating
a family	of four
now,	
a couple	with two older kids
at the bar	
it's	what I swallow
what hops	inside me.
Maybe	these birds
	aren't
crows	at all.
Maybe	these birds
don't	want to settle for
	scraps

Maybe they're deaf   to the feint-hearted
apology of   the manager
that may or may not
arrive   before the restaurant
                            closes
and the offer
for
a free drink   dilutes.
                            My hunger holds
between
clenched teeth.
                            My hunger
a camel   at the edge of desert
mirage of oasis   in plain view.
Maybe   there's something else
Maybe they're   asps
                            maybe
                            pythons
The hostess   snakes
through
the angled aisles   and weaves
the lone man   three parties back
and finds
him
a cozy table   at the picture window
Licked
lips   compressed
lips
Lipsticked   lips
Fat lips   The patrons
who are seated
and served   chew
swallow,   their plates
emptying   emptying
                            as their stomachs distend
I
swallow too   to keep
the bile   from rising
to keep   my feet
steady   steady
                            as I go

```
back                              outside
and
stand                             on the cobbled sidewalk
The birds                         dying
The birds                         felled.
Something stirring                from the ashes
The birds                         rising
again
all mouth                         I'm
an often-served                   meal
at the public table the hot ash
of their hate
I swallow                         the cold night air
instead
of
the chef's special                written in chalk
on a black easel
I swallow                         and swallow
and the birds                     perched
wings extended                    on the verge
                                  of
                                  flight
I                                 now
                                  a mouth newly employed
instead of eating                 with a knife
in one hand                       and a fork
in the other                      I consume this
hostess' hate                     with my eyes
and carve out                     salt-cured curses
from my                           mother
tongue
and serve them                    cold and loudly
from where                        I stand.
I cannot digest                   these birds
any                               longer.
```

The All-Saints, XX, Overeaters Support Group (meeting #18)

First we talk about watermelons—
a modern, American reference
to family picnics, seed-spitting contests,
abating a thirst for summer love
by eating weightless pink flesh.

Then our study of the Greek myths
seeps through our tongues as pomegranates
are hurled onto our invisible
table, pungent olives, golden
apples, blood oranges, Medea.

Someone comments on sorrow
as an appetite suppressant—
death provokes fasting, in some cases
a strict diet of bitter remembrance
until the taste for life returns.

Others blurt out hors d'oeuvres stories
at the theatre, cocktail parties, movies.
And at weddings, how the cake is too sweet,
the toasting champagne always falls flat
by the time the waiter reaches their glasses.

We discuss the reluctant meals we swallow
when there is no money leftover after rent:
white bread that's three days old, noodles,
peanut butter without the jelly,
lentil soups with rice, bags of popcorn.

No one mentions why we come here,
the way we slide into our chairs, batter
stealing home, without notice, without
admitting that we want to soufflé
our bodies from landfills to temples.

We laugh at the staple of fairy tales:
apples poisoned by jealousy,
gingerbread houses, cooked goose,
blackbird pies, cooling porridge, stone
soup, beanstalks that lead to giant feasts.

Then someone mumbles a fable about
the seven sins but I am too far
away to hear it, a joke that
I don't understand because I can't
get past gluttony and avarice.

Finally, a discourse on Vegas:
the incandescent dramas, all night
slots and sex, currency exchange
and love, how breakfast is served
at these twenty-four hour buffets.

It's about choice, I say. The use of buffet
is to speak of selection; the hierarchy
of egg dishes, for example:
how Benedict is better than poached,
the sauce enhancing the runny yolk.

No, a voice calls out from the circle:
Buffet is all-you-can-eat,
it's tasting a lot of everything,
eating it all. Freedom and acceptance.
It's taking the whole world into your heart.

The hour is up and I am hungry.

Self-Portrait (Inside the Movie Theater, Near the Santa Cruz Mountains, Near the County Limits)(You Are There, Expecting To Glimpse a Pivotal Moment In the Life Of Ron Stallworth's Infiltration In To the __ ___ ___.)(*BlacKkKlansman* Gifts You With Memory: Reminds You Of Your Own Experiences With the ___ During Your Journalism Days That You Had Long Buried.)(and It puts Forth an Alternative Context In Which To View _____ and _____ —"Celebrated" Movies That You Were Once Required To Watch At Degree-Conferring Institutions.)(Idea: Maybe History Does Not Have To Be Solely Viewed Through the Eyes Of Racist America, Put Forth By the Dominant Culture.)(Idea: This Movie Is a Permission Slip To Write More About Racism In Your Home Country, These United States Of America.)(Idea: Maybe Schools Should Show *BlacKkKlansman* In Place Of the Other Two Films, Like a Permanent Substitute Teacher) (At Once It's 2018 As the Story Unfolds Before You On the Silver Screen and Yet You're In 198-, 198-, 198-, 198-, 199-, 199-, 199-, 199-, 200-, 200-, 200-, 201-, 201- and All the Times You've Seen _____ Advertised Or Shown On TV In the Intervening Years)(Because This Meets the Definition Of 'Appropriate Entertainment')(a Year Since Charlottesville?)(and Still the Confederate Monuments Largely Stand) (Because These Meet the Definition Of "Right" Side of History)(As If Slavery Were an Exaggeration, As If the 1619 Project Were Based On a Misunderstanding)(As You Watch Spike Lee's Film, Your Head Aches, Your Heart Sprints As You Remember. Watching Hooded Men On Horseback, Sweat Dampens the Shirt On Your Back)(a Loop, But Fragmentary)(You Struggle With PTSD, (For Years)(Not All Of the Memories Are Complete and Not All Of the Memories Are Consecutive:) (1. Spike Lee Opens With the Expansive Scene In _____, You Know the One, Where Scarlett Wades Through a Thick Swath Of Injured Soldiers Lying On the Ground and a Confederate Flag Blows In the Breeze. (2018))(2. ___ _____ Set Up In the 1980s For _____ To Play On Multiple Screens At His Theatre At CNN 6 In Atlanta. (It Ran Continuously From 1987-2000))(You Saw the Marquee In 198- When You First Came To Atlanta As An Intern and Ended Up Interviewing a _____ That Summer; and Years Later, When You Moved Back To Georgia. (198-)(199-))(In 201-, the Guinness Book Of World Records Estimated _____ As the Highest Grossing Film In History) (Adjusting for Inflation)(Clocking In At $3.4 Billion)(Margaret Mitchell won the National Book Award for it, in 193-, the Pulitzer Prize in 193-; and in 193-, her book was made into an Oscar-winning film starring Clark Gable and Vivien Leigh.)(3. The First Time You Spoke

To ___ ____, You Were an Intern For the _____, and You Worked Out Of a Northern Suburb Bureau. ____ Proclaimed Himself To Be the Grand ____ Of the _____ ____ _____)(Your Feminist Metro Editor Had Given You the Assignment; To Call This Man and Some Government Officials and Write a Story About the Upcoming ___ Rally) (Your Editor Was 26 At the Time and Declared In Response To Other People's Doubts, "No One Tells Me Who I Send To Cover a Story.")(She Looked At You and Said, "You Can Do It.")(The City Of Lawrenceville Had Given the __ __ __ a Permit To Gather and March.)(The ____ Was Haggling About the Use Of a Bullhorn)(The Summer of 198- Brought the Democratic National Convention To Nearby Atlanta As Well; the Area Was Gaining Attention)(You Picked Up the Boxy Black Phone At Your Messy Desk and Dialed. _____ Caught Your Name As ____ and You Didn't Correct Him, His Voice Chatty As He Described His Disdain and Hatred For People Of Color and Jews (Denied the Holocaust), Blamed These Groups For America's Decline)(You Scribbled Notes Into Your Reporter's Pad, the Receiver Cradled Between Your Shoulder and Ear) (The Next Day, Your Feminist Metro Editor Thanks You For the Good Work, and Assigns a Follow Up Story About the Bullhorn To Someone Else)(The Following Saturday,)(After __ ____, Convicted Of the 1958 Bombing Of a Black Birmingham Church, Concluded His Rant,) (Another Reporter Who Was Also Covering the Rally (Your Friend & Mentor, Kathy) Saw You Standing Near the Police and the Protestors (Who Outnumbered the ____ Three-To-One)("Do You Want To Meet ___?" She Asked))(When You Said Yes, She Disappeared Among the Throng Of White Robed _____ Shouting Their Hate.)(She Returned With _____, and Pointed To You and Said To Him, Sternly,)("She's the Reporter You Talked To On the Phone. She's American, Just Like Me.") (_____ Opened His Mouth and Closed It (Twice) and Turned Away Without Uttering a Single Word (198-))(4. Early In *BlacKkKlansman*, White Supremacist Dr. Kennebrew Beauregard (Played By ____ ____) Spews Vitriol.)(Behind Him, _____ Plays, Sometimes Running Over His Face. (2018))(5. In College You Were Forced To Watch _____ As an Example Of Early Cinematic Achievement.) (You Will Remember Your Classmates' Laughter For the Rest Of Your Life. (198-))(6. At One Point Early In the Film There Is Discussion Between the Undercover Policeman and the _____ about Affirmative Action, Immigration, Crime. Though It Is a Film Set In the 1970s, Most Of the Rhetoric Sounds Contemporary)(Post 201-, Post Election.)

(A Short Time Later, There Is a Prescient Yet Comedic Moment When One Policeman Tells Another That ____ ____'s Goal Is To Have a ____ Sympathizer Serving As President, Living In the White House. (2018)) (But Didn't President ____ First Fill That Promise, When He Screened _____ In the White House In 191-?)(7. In 1970s Dollars, the Cost Of a Year-Long Membership In the National __ ___ ___ Was $10 In Addition To a $15 Local Chapter Fee)(Robes and Hoods Were Not Included))(8. A Second Chance To Talk To ____ _____ Arose, Several Months Later. You Tried To Convince the Florida Patriarchal Newsroom You Could Do the Job.)(At the Larger Newspaper In Georgia You'd Just Left, You'd Been Spoiled By Your Feminist Metro Editor. You'd Interned At This Newspaper In a Small Town In ____ Florida the Year Before, But In the Fourteen Months It Took For You To Graduate From College and Work Your Way Back, There Had Been a Regime Change.)(The Newsroom Had Received Notice That the ____ Was Coming To Florida) (To Towns Due North Of Your Offices)(That ____ ____ Might Be In Attendance)(You Stood At the Threshold Of the New Executive Metro Editor's Office, and Volunteered)("He Knows Me," You'd Said. "I'd Like To Go.")(The New Executive Metro Editor Laughed and Said No, Cited Safety Concerns.)("There Are Going To Be a Million Cops. That'll Be the Safest Spot In All Of Florida," You'd Said.)(You Voiced Your Concern That White Supremacists Were Dictating To Newsrooms How To Cover Them)(He Laughed Again and Said Something About Free Speech, Free Country)(You'd Said, "But Free Speech Isn't Hate Speech.")(Other Reporters Were Assigned To Cover Those Stories.) (Your Classmate Rolled Her Eyes At You When the Assignments Were Handed Down.)(A Month Or So Passed, and Your Classmate Told You As You Walked To Your Cars In the Employee Parking Lot One Evening That She Had Had Enough,)(and Accepted a Job At a Much Larger Newspaper In Your Shared Home State (198-))(You Left For IL Five Months Later)(And Soon After Saw Three Crosses Burning By the Interstate)(Burning What Was Left Of Your Hope For Change) (Forever)(Forever, Three Crosses Will Burn At the End Of Memory Lane) With Bathroom Mirror, Movie Hall, Mountain View, CA—2018

God, I can't look.
God, I can't look away.

Unanswered, Untranslatable

On her mother's tongue, the word is "andho"
blind unseeing, blind's undoing. Blind blind.

In her mother tongue, the word's embedded
in the dim, inside the well deep with night.

"Andho-kar" is darkness, synonymous
with a sky scorned by stars, emptied of moon.

Memory is praise and plundered, rued, like
a yew tree fallen to blight. You see our

weather as foregone conclusion but berth
is not a birth except when it is one.

((Haibun) Self-Portrait (Near the Halogen Stove, Near the Blonde Wooden Cutting-Board In the Shape Of a Tar Heel Foot, the Iconic Symbol of NC)(and Symbol of UNC-CH)(a Gift From Her, Your Visiting Mother)(It Is Only When Your Mother Visits In This Way That the Tiny Granny Smith Apple Slices (Tart & Crisp Down To the Last Molecule) Reveal Themselves—Her Stories, That Is)(You Stand In the Radius Of Her Sight As She Inspects the Kaacha-Kala and Directs You To Peel & Cube the Plantains For the Curry)(You Oblige, and Keep Your Eyes First On the Bunch of Green Bananas (That, Together Resemble the Bottom Of a Spring Basket, a Basket Without Handles)) (Then the Peel As You Carve Away With a Large Stainless-Steel Knife, Separating the Newly-Green Skin From the Dense Yellow Starch)(You Had Picked Up a Blackened Ripe Bunch At the Market But She had Taken Them Out Of the Cart and Replaced Them)(You Do Not Look At Her Hands, Gnarling Into Bonsai From Rheumatoid Arthritis)(You Try Not To Consider That She Has Not Eaten This Dish In Years)(That Your Baba No Longer Cuts the Vegetables For Her)(That His Ailments Have Changed Him Irrevocably)(You Listen Carefully As She Speaks Of Your Baba, Her Husband Of More Than a Half-Century)('He Would Love This Curry, It Is Such a Delicacy')(You Smile)('It Takes Too Long To Make This If You Can't Separate the Peel At the Beginning')('You Can Slice the Plantains and Plunge Them Into Boiling Water But the Taste Is Lost')(You Begin To Comprehend As She Explains How To Slice the Green Skin)('Don't Leave So Much Flesh On the Skin! Cut Closer! Cut More Perfectly')(You Finish This Task and Go To Throw Away the Shards Of Peel and)(She Says No)(She Switches Topics and Begins Again With a Story About the Last Time She Was In Baguiati, Before He Died)(How the Young Girl Who Travelled From the Village To Work in the Kolkata Enclave, Never Discarded the Skins)(How She Chopped Finely the Skin, and Made Mocha (Hard CH))(Standard Bengali Fare)('What's Her Name?')('I Don't Know Anymore. I'll Never See Her Again.')(You Cube the Last Section Of the Kaach-Kala and Remember Your Dadu, Your Ma's Baba, Using the Very Same Word In a Different Context)(Plantain As Slang For Nothing, As In Being Left Unrewarded After a Difficult Task)(She Asks You To Save Some Of the Diced Vegetable For Later)(You Pour the Bowl of Cubed Plantain Into the Boiling Water)(She Scolds You For Not Listening As You Try To Wash the Green Sap From Your Sticky Fingers)(She Scolds Herself For Not Reminding You Sooner)('You're Supposed To Oil Your Hands Before You Handle the Plantains, They Leech If You Cook Them Before They Are Ripe')(You Have No Luck With Soap)

('Cut Some Lemon and Squeeze Them Over Your Hand')(She Turns To Leave)('Smash Some Cardamom, Black Peppercorns and Cinnamon Stick In the Mortar & Pestle Just Before You Turn Off the Heat')('Thaar Pore Namiye Deh')(Bangla Phrase That Roughly Translates To 'Take It Down')(Referring To Taking The Karai Off the Uu-Noon)) With Fun House Reflection (In Chrome Faucet—No.—, US, No. America, 202-)

God, I have to remember.
God, I have to write this down.
God, I can never find a pen.

Why I ___

I ____ to present an end product for all of the day's troubles. I ____
to change the color of the peas in the rice pilaf. I ____ to discover
if the toasted cumin seeds will mask the smell of the m___ searing
in the frying pan. I ____ to see the kitchen ghost again, my gr____ aunt
who died because of a bride burning, a dowry d____h in the kitchen,
long before I was born. I ____ to bring friends to my table. I ____ to
feed strangers. I ____ to raise money for the homeless, to help the ones
without a kitchen of their own. I ____ to displace my anger, and my grief.
I ____ to remember how I loved to ____ as a child, before my mother
began to look me over toe to top and find fault with my weight. I ____
to teach my daughter how to brown the butter, how to ch____ on the
paneer by substituting ricotta cheese, as my mother used to do. I ____ as
a way to measure the hour. I ____ to remember my grandmother's face
illuminated by the coals glowing from the open mouth of the clay oven.
I ____ to travel back in time, to a moment when I was perfectly happy
but didn't know it then. I ____ to travel to distant lands. I ____ to learn
by doing, to understand the mechanics of a mandolin, how the peeler
separates a vegetable from its skin, how a grater reduces a marbled mass
of blue cheese to edible rubble. I ____ to stem the hunger I cannot ever
fully erase; I ____ to ____. I ____to feed my daughters. I ____ to ____
the domestic fowl strutting by the barn whose opinions on the w____her
I don't understand—but consume anyway. I ____ to avoid ____ing the
migrating birds loudly announcing their departure. I ____ when I'm
starving. I ____ when I am full and cannot even imagine ____ing what
I'm about to make. I ____ to honor the farmers, their toil, their tangles
with the seasons and the storms to bring my ingredients to market. I
____ to remember my cousin who died too soon and his fondness for
Indo-Chinese takeout. I ____ so I have something to scour later, so I can
render the utensils pristine. I ____ to remember all of my kin. I ____ to
witness the miracle of translucency, how the glass noodles are at once
transparent and opaque after a brief bath in boiling water. I ____ as an act
of standing still and picturing how the future will taste. I ____ as an act
of moving quickly, b____ing the clock on the stainless steel face
of the microwave, meeting a deadline, bringing a certain taste to fruition.
I ____ to feed the demons of loss within me, to offer them a free meal, a
moment for them to stop gnawing on my grieving heart.
   I ____ to dispel the silence in the house. I ____ to carry on a three act
play with the stove and the fridge and spice cabinets in supporting roles. I
____ because we must all ____. I ____ to offer prayer to a universe that

is largely invisible to my naked eyes. I ____ to remember those hyper-thin men who ____ed for 500 at my uncle's wedding, how they were addressed as Thakur, God, how they smiled as they lit the gas stoves and conducted the symphony of large woks and layered curries with metal tongs. I ____ to become a short-order ____ and withstand the outside world's demands. I ____ so that I can look out the window at the willow tree as I wait for the onions to transform from purple to golden brown. I ____ as a way to prove my worth as a ____ and as a ____. I ____ so that I can sing-song the words of my youth that I want to say, without appearing insane: biriyani, fricassee, turmeric, tureen, all the lyrics to *A Spoonful of Sugar*. I ____ to witness transformation, and transfiguration. I ____ to avoid acidity and indigestion that comes with store bought foods. I ____ knowing the risk that my experiments could lead to food poisoning, a trip to the emergency room, an injection to stave off vomiting and nausea. I ____ to stuff my birds of doubts with the tastes of successes, the delicacies of fish masala, the steamed rice cakes twice the size of a sand dollar, and the whole milk cucumber raita just so. It doesn't matter what I ____, as long as I try. It doesn't matter, the oil splattering the stovetop, the counter, my clothes and occasionally my fingers. All that matters is that I keep trying. I ____ as though it is my last day to have such a task. I ____ to demonstrate I am capable of love. I ____ to demonstrate that I want to be loved. I ____ as though it is the last day I will ever ____ or want to.

((Haibun) Self-Portrait (Near the 1960 Winter Olympics Village, Near Lake Tahoe)(But Not Near These Locations At All)(Near the Primordial Parent Aspen (Unlike the Old Woman Who Lived In a Shoe, This Mother Has Always Known What To Do)(Prolifically Propagate) and Also Near the Hometown Of the All-Knowing Fruit) (In a Time When Virtual Reality Is Synonymous With Reality)(In the State Of Poetry & Dream) the Faces In the Gallery (Some Ruddy and Brisk, Some Shining In Their Desert Swelter) Some Familiar Like Your Own Reflection But Most Are Beautiful New Tidings In the Rookery)(You are Told You Are a Birder, You Are Told This Is a Birding Camp)(You Learn After You Settle On Your Perch That One Of the Birds Studied Is Going To Be You)(Some Birders Rely Heavily On the Eyes, Never Disinterested But Still Detached, While Others Murmur Encouragement As They Help You Adjust Your Binocular Lens)(Some Elevate the Discussion Beyond Habitat and Caloric Consumption) (Some Whisper-Speak Of the Famous Parakeet Who Has Flown,)(the Parakeet Is Always the First To Go)(Others Ululate About the Balance Of the Mead Moon, How Honeyed Its Gaze As It Varnishes the Wings Of the Night Owl's)(But Often the Rose Light Leaves the Starlings and Sparrow Feeling Beaky)(Talk, Talk, Talk)(You Wonder About Your Grandfather's Practice of Augury (But the Moment Is Fleeting As You Picture the Kingfishers, Peacocks and Swifts You Encountered in Once Upon a Time India)(You Try to Spell Ornithomancy In Your Head As Someone Chirps Out Of Turn About Romulus and His Vision Of a Kettle Of Vultures Before He Won the City That Bears His Name)(a Pair of Steller's Jay Lay Now Siege On the Actual Branch Outside Your Window, a Raven Pours His Beak Into the Pool)(the Oldest Bird In the Group, So Pleased At the (Bouquet's)(Convocation's)(Muster's) Progress, Proposes To Alter the Anthology's Title From 'Birding For Beginners' To 'Intermediate Birding')(You Remember Five Years Have Passed Since the Height Of the Drought, the Wreck of Lupine Had Grown Where Tahoe Should Have Been)(Ecclesiastical Bees Congregating, Speaking In One Tongue)(You Remember the Floods the Following Year, How the Drowned Lupine Cast the Lake Into An Undulating Shade Of Roman Blue)(You Wonder If You'll Ever Fly Again)(Outside the Internet, On the Ether))—At Divination Conference, No.—, US, 202-

God, they say you reside in every living thing.
God, their songs tell me you're the ghost inside machines.

Acknowledgments

Grateful acknowledgment is made to the editors of the following publications where these poems, some of which have been subsequently revised, originally appeared:

Omnium Gatherum (publication of Community of Writers): While the mayfly bombards the river reeds…

Tin House: Sounding Off

Tule Review: Aunt-By-Marriage

Concis: Unanswered, untranslatable

Anastasia Maps (chapbook), Finishing Line Press: In this game of Sorry, you never apologize

The Raleigh Review: Untitled Western Country Song… (nominated for Best New American Poetry)

The Atlanta Review: Raga

West Trestle Review: Departure Terminal

Panorama: Self-Portrait With Child

Panorama: Self-Portrait Outside the U.S. District

Press 53: On Sadness

Pratichi Magazine: Routes

Rattle: Though the Stars Walk Backward

Under The Volcano Anthology: Measuring the Weight of your Smile & Scratch

North American Review: The All-Saints, XX, Overeaters Support Group (also nominated for Pushcart Prize, and later published in *Why To These Rocks* anthology)

Enormous gratitude to my champions at Finishing Line Press: Leah & Kevin Maines, Christen Kincaid, Mimi David. Thank you for your efforts to bring this book into existence.

Thanks for everything Reiko Davis at DeFiore & Co., and for the incredible support of Elizabeth Rosner, Shikha Malaviya and Ewa Chrusciel. Love to the extended Laskar, Chakravarty, Dasgupta and Sen families, especially Joy Laskar & Gauri Sen.

Thank you to the multitude of friends, colleagues and teachers, family and chosen family for your unconditional support over the years. This book would not be possible without you. Special love to Anjini & Ellora & Devrani Laskar, Ru & Kimmy Sen, Nabin Laskar, Elizabeth Stark & Angie Powers, Sejal Patel, Korinne Lassiter, Parna & Tesha Sengupta, Dorothy Hearst, Linda Hosek, Karineh Mahdessian, Zeyn Joukhadar, Deborah Krainin, Pete & Patricia Apostolakis, Gloria & Juergen Hoefler, Tanya & Jay Kruse, Kathy & Dean Brewer, Shankar & Ruma Sengupta, Faith Hoople, Robin Holtson, Eric & Helen Graben, Vi Pham, Anjoli Roy, Sunanda McGarvey, my VONA family, Aya de Leon, Brett Hall Jones & Lisa Alvarez at Community of Writers, Luchina Fisher, Lane Mitchell, Lucille Clifton, Elmaz Abinader, Molly Fisk, Samiya Bashir, Kazim Ali, Blas Falconer, Evie Shockley, Paul Muldoon, Ellen Bass, Monique Truong, Brenda Hillman, Robert Hass, Sharon Olds, Matthew Webb, Amanda White, David Ishaya Osu, Nicole Sealey, Amy Louise Murray.

Thinking of the ones who would be especially proud today, but are gone too soon: Pranab K. Sen, Amulya L. & Renu C. Laskar, J.R. & Nilima Dasgupta, Kalyani Sen, Susan Freiburg.

Devi S. Laskar is a native of Chapel Hill, North Carolina, and holds an MFA from Columbia University. *The Atlas of Reds and Blues* (Counterpoint Press, 2019)— winner of the Asian/Pacific American Award for Literature and the Crook's Corner Book Prize) is her debut novel. It was selected by The Georgia Center for the Book as a book "All Georgians Should Read," long-listed for the DSC Prize in South Asian Literature, and long-listed for the Golden Poppy Award presented by the California Independent Booksellers Alliance. *The Atlas of Reds and Blues* was named by *The Washington Post* as one of the best books of 2019, and has garnered praise in *Time* magazine, *The San Francisco Chronicle, The Guardian*, and elsewhere.

In 2022, Mariner Books published Laskar's second novel, *Circa*. This novel was a GOOP Book Club selection. Her third novel, *Midnight, At The War,* is forthcoming from Mariner Books.

A former newspaper reporter, Laskar is now a poet, photographer, artist, and novelist based in California. Laskar also holds an MA in South Asian Studies from the University of Illinois at Urbana-Champaign, and BAs in English and journalism from UNC-Chapel Hill. In 2017, Finishing Line Press published two poetry chapbooks, *Gas & Food, No Lodging* and *Anastasia Maps*. In 2019, Aunt Lute Press published *Graffiti*, a mixed-genre anthology produced by writers of color that she co-edited. In 2021, Madville Publishing published *Taboos & Transgressions*, a mixed-genre anthology that focuses on breaking the rules that she co-edited.

Self-Portraits Ex Machina is her debut collection of poetry.

www.ingramcontent.com/pod-product-compliance
Lightning Source LLC
Chambersburg PA
CBHW030059170426
43197CB00010B/1596